JANUARY RAIN

For Timothy,
With very best wishes.
Good luck with your own
creative endeavors.

Danny
June, 1998
Huntington, NY

The Nicholas Roerich Poetry Prize

is an annual first-book competition sponsored by the
Nicholas Roerich Museum in New York City

1988
The Volcano Inside by David Dooley

1989
Without Asking by Jane Ransom

1990
Death, But at a Good Price by Chris Semansky

1991 co-winners
The Buried Houses by David Mason
Desire's Door by Lee McCarthy

1992
30 Miles from J-Town by Amy Uyematsu

1993
House Without a Dreamer by Andrea Hollander Budy

1994
Counterpoint by David Alpaugh

1995
The Silent Partner by Greg Williamson

1996
Infidelities by Elise Paschen

Each volume of the Nicholas Roerich Poetry Prize Library
is in print and available from:
Story Line Press, Three Oaks Farm, Brownsville, OR 97327

JANUARY RAIN

Daniel Anderson

Daniel Anderson (signature)

Story Line Press ✦ 1997

Published by Story Line Press, Inc.
Three Oaks Farm, Brownsville, OR 97327

This publication was made possible thanks in part to the generous support of the Nicholas Roerich Museum, the Andrew W. Mellon Foundation, and our individual contributors.

Book design by M. Rae Thompson

Library of Congress Cataloging-in-Publication Data
Anderson, Daniel, 1964–
    January rain / Daniel Anderson.
        p.   cm.
    "1997 co-winner, Nicholas Roerich Poetry Prize."
    ISBN 1-885266-54-5 (pbk.)
    1. Title.
PS3551.N3584J36   1997
811'.54—dc21
                                      97-23542
                                        CIP

Acknowledgments

I would like to express my gratitude to the following journals in which some of these poems first appeared:

> *The Formalist:* "The Nightly News"
> *The Journal:* "Camp Chase Confederate Cemetery"
> *The New Republic:* "Buddy Check"
> *Poetry:* "Epilogue," "Executive Geochrone"
> *Raritan:* "The Last Resort," "A Possum's Tale"
> *Sewanee Theological Review:* "The Essay Writers,"
> "Standard Time"
> *The Southern Review:* "To Charcot: A Letter Never Posted,"
> "Dontophobic"
> *Southwest Review:* "The Last Day of School."

"The Dog Laments His Day" originally appeared under the title "Domi Solus" in *Unleashed: Poems by Writers' Dogs* (Crown Publishing).

I would like to thank the New Jersey State Council on the Arts for a generous grant in 1995. I would also like to express my gratitude to Jo, Michael, and Phil Borack, Brian Fleury, Rachel Hadas, Anthony Hecht, John Hollander, Andrew Hudgins, Erin McGraw, Cheri Peters, and Wyatt Prunty. For their sustaining friendship, advice, and patience, I would especially like to thank Philip Stephens, and Greg Williamson. "The Last Resort" is dedicated to Anthony Hecht.

"But how can I hope to explain myself here; and yet, in some dim, random way, explain I must, else all these chapters might be naught." —Herman Melville, *Moby Dick*

Table of Contents

I

II

III

IV

Part I

Standard Time

The church's spire, the courthouse clock,
And all the slanted roofs that line the square,
Of dime store, bank, and Mitchell's Shoe Repair,
Have joined their silhouettes to interlock
Against the evening's cold cornflower sky.
The velvet counter-darkness of the street
Seems painted by the sly hand of Magritte
To stump the mind and its bewildered eye.

A failing light. The growing zodiac.
A windfall hour spent. Each leaf-lined yard
Is cloaked in tones of cobblestone and slate
As we discover in our turning back
An early dusk we cannot disregard,
A change we never quite anticipate.

The Essay Writers

One threading fingers through her hair remarks,
Off in the margin of a vacant page,
How much the clusters of catalpa trees
Across the quad sway like anemones.

Another time she might receive an A
For her insightful gift of likening
If she were asked to contrast and compare;
Her slouch implies that I have been unfair.

As ten great authors on a poster fade
And she begins to ruminate among
Gun-metal grays and simulated grains,
Fresh blackboard slates and plots of water stains

That creep beneath the plaster like disease,
A better teacher might convince them all
There is a far more lovely place that spreads
Beneath their ball-points and dull pencil leads.

But teacher is preoccupied today
Remarking to himself how there exists
A solemness in watching them create
That even he cannot articulate.

Late September in the Field

The year is running out as it always does
And tacitly the beech trees tip their hands
While jade is draining from their drying leaves.
Still hidden vaguely in its olive loft,
A limb-line choir of crows rehearses
Its repertoire and short-list hymnal of
Complaint. The taller, bobbing spears of grain,
Awash in late September light, are coaxed
To blonde, and summer once again is poised
Upon the verge of afterthought. *Recall!*
Recall! the tin-can alto crooners chant
As sun-streams trickle through the woods to print
A latticework of shadow on the grass.
The inventory tallies itself.
Although we know such evidence evolves
To dull and pencilled skeletons of vine
And forestries of bone and brittle ghosts,
A nail glides down a perfumed wrist; two lips
Immaculately tremble through their kiss.
And these are not the first thoughts on our minds.

A Possum's Tale

He's hauled himself out from a stranger place,
Unnoticed and in turn unnoticing
Of highbeams drifting down the cul-de-sac
Or shafts of streetlight angling through the limbs.
He makes his way, hunched deep into himself,
A tarnished silver creature bearing down
On corn silk, melon rinds, and celery stalks
Dissolving into compost where they fell
One afternoon beside the barbecue.
Three children heading in from kick-the-can,
Their mothers having called them home from play,
Have cornered him beneath a picnic bench.
They pitch small stones and jab him with a stick,
Mistake his grin for a half-sarcastic smirk,
And meddle with his naked, coiled tail.
Enduring simply what he must endure,
He focuses the black beads of his eyes
On tufts of grass and dandelion thorns.
Perhaps he mutters something to himself
When, racing off at last, the boys depart
And he is left to needle into night,
Beneath the neighborhood's display of light,
While windows, like paintings on their easels, bear
Rare glimpses into unfamiliar lives.
Through bronze and copper rooms dark figures pass,

Their liquid shadows trailing after them.
On someone's parlor chandelier glass drops
Cascade like waters from a fountainhead.
Three houses down, high in a gable pane,
A sewing mannequin admires her gown
While he finds loveliness in scabs of moss,
Inspects the gunwales of a garbage can,
And drags behind him in his quiet wake
A strangeness only he can comprehend.

The Last Resort

The slatted chairs in rank and file await
    A rising tourist tide
    Of cars from out-of-state
And contemplate a vacant waterside

Where six days prior to this threat of showers
    Angled umbrellas chased
    And courted like sunflowers
The sun that cold-front harbingers erased,

And glistening bathers bivouacked with oils,
    Picnic, hats, paperbacks,
    And bright reflecting foils
To whet the edge of daylight's flashing ax.

But now the bas-relief is rendered thin,
    Its surface sanded down
    Where terry cloth and skin
Once shaped a human sculpture on this ground.

The boardwalk groans; a sea gull pipes farewells,
    And like a paper kite
    Above the pewter swells
Seems tugged by a distant thread from left to right.

Between us there is little to be said.
        The car is glumly packed
        With duffel bags and dread
While bellhops recreate the final act

Of some continuous, congenial play
        In which the audience
        Is always cast away
As Eden tidies up its innocence.

Though much of this is sad—the lawless wind,
        The foam of knuckling waves—
        We must not now rescind
Our joys because this morning misbehaves.

If grinding tide and breeze with its raw rush
        Could part their lips to speak
        They'd tell us in a hush
Such lives are rented merely by the week.

Executive Geochrone

a map shop in December

The local peddler of geographies
Has hung a world which darkens by degrees
And lightens, also, as a sine wave glides
Over islands, continents, and still seas.

Occasionally browsers stop to ask
The idle clerk about the sine wave's task,
Though anyone could patiently observe
Its job is first to mask and then unmask

This planet with a corresponding light
To dusks that fall and mornings that ignite.
And calmly as that map grinds down its days
We view our lives as from a placid height.

Beyond the store's plate glass the first snows drift,
Blanketing streets like ash. The awnings shift
And signposts swagger in rank bursts of wind.
On Christmas Eve, in search of one last gift,

A globe, perhaps, a flag, or travel book
To gather dust in someone's inglenook,
Each customer compares the worlds he wants
As Argentina's turquoise buttonhook

Is cloaked in evening not yet reaching here.
A blue wine spills over this hemisphere,
Has washed across Bermuda's jagged coasts,
And hints of our own nightfall edging near.

One sees in this illuminated chart
Both time and place made graspable by art
And how each unveiled strip of morning light
Is balanced by a darkling counterpart.

Tomorrow when the presents are all passed
Around the living room, a low broadcast
Of caroling will chime the morning out;
The ornaments, which once seemed colorfast,

Will hang less brightly. Silences will stoke
The ghosts that January grays provoke,
And all soft essences that charged the air,
Of pine bough, holly wreath, and chimney smoke

Will be remembrancers of what has gone,
While through the sash that frames a snowy lawn
We'll watch a day that darkens by degrees
And witness something darker drawing on.

The Bitter End

Summoned from a fresh page
Of winter, and finished with a stovepipe hat,
The snowman started life in middle age,
Bald and running to fat.

In a corner of the yard
Beneath an ice-encrusted pine tree tassel,
Honor-bound and dauntless, he stood guard
Over the frozen castle

Built also by a child
On the unshovelled morning after the storm.
He lingers there, content to wait, in a mild
And vaguely human form,

Dissolving into the mud.
He's shed his scarf and dropped his walking cane,
Endured the soft and intermittent thud
Of January rain,

And still maintains his grinning
While comprehending nothing of his demise,
Not the dangling corncob nor the thinning
Sockets of his eyes.

He makes the slow return
From gutter stream through glittering brook to sea
With relatively small or no concern
    For his own misery;

He's never been known to grouse
About warm weather or his loosening bones,
And all day long he's faced this lonely house
    Cracking his smile of stones.

Part II

After a Long Winter

Across the once confectionery yards,
Where glazes of rock candy and meringue
Rounded the contours of our suburbanside,
Rope hammocks drape and wickets run their course,
The lawn chairs like perennials return,
And in the waxing fan of light-shine on
Their deck, the next-door daughters sun themselves,
Gossip, and drink iced tea from mason jars.
Their words which drift across the picket fence
Are intertwined with birdsong, rasps of saws,
And the chatterings of a dozen sprinkler storms.
These things one hears while condensation grows
Like seed pearls on a silver can of beer
Or as blue swallows dot the power line.
We've lost our grasp on winter now as this,
A season of forgiveness, light, and lust
Drives daylong in its own moist hum. The girls,
Who mostly talk about a boy named Jeff,
And their father, wrangling with the mower chain,
Carry on as though it had never been
Anything else. Without much thought we learn
Sometimes to pardon what has brought us grief,
As one might casually remark how high
Along the bank of honeysuckle vines
Those wild roses hang like April snow.

Snipe Hunt

Golden evening, August light
Sifted down and glazed
The cellar door where I was told
To wait. They said emerald sparks
Would flicker when their bellies
Scraped across the road,
And squinting into the citrine dusk
That's what I expected
When my four cousins
Rounded the corner of the house
Clapping madly for me
To get cracking, sending me
Frenzied into the street
As I whacked two sticks
Hard together and barked,
Snipe! Snipe! Snipe! Snipe!
They dragged me to the churchyard
Where they swore they'd seen
A glimmer in the brush.
They whistled me back
To dig beneath the porch
Where I thrust my head
Into a musty hole,
Open-mouthed and panting,
And swallowed down a web

Splayed across the black hatch.
I jerked back and slammed
My head on a joist.
It's always funny until
Someone gets hurt and then,
Of course, it's really funny.
But I'd been cruising for it.
All summer I nagged,
Needled them over an edge
Until they finally gave me
The attention that I'd been
Dumb as a bucket to beg them for.

But once is not a lesson learned
And almost ten years later,
In bed with a first love,
I couldn't let drop
The rumor that I heard
How she, drunk on gin at a party,
The year before we met,
Made love with two boys
While others watched.
Strangely laughing at first,
She scolded my curiosity,
Denied it. Then she stopped

And rising through the flesh
I held to mine was a slow
Shuddering of muscle
Deepening with gasps and heaves
Until she snapped out,
I wasn't making love!

Almost every day I hear
A new joke where I work.
Today, Arthur stopped by
To ask me if I knew
How long it takes
To make a woman come.
He flapped his hand and cackled out,
Who cares? Of course. Every day I think,
Of course, I should have known.

It's February now
And this one thing I know:
These cataracts of ice along the walk,
This pigeon-colored snow,
Will never rinse away.
And when I watch this winter melt,
Fold into the fields,
When gardens pucker and burst

With eggplant, corn, and yellow squash,
I will be addled once again,
How everything resolves itself
If only through an end.

Yorick's Skull

Scrap. Scrap. Scrap. The dog and I go tramping
Through the woods. Sometimes the pace is fierce,
With both our noses pointed to the ground,
Though he is somewhat further off the trail,
And I am not enraptured by the scents
Of markings and decay. One day we made
The turn we'd made at least—I'll swear—
Three dozen times before, when he stopped cold,
Hunkered low, raised his hackles, then tip-toed
To a mound of gray and rotting bones,
Which he circled twice before he lifted up
His leg, then scampered off. Nothing much
Was left except some ribs, a spine, and half
A grinning, hollow head. No telling what it was—
A groundhog or raccoon. But that dog didn't care
Too much. *Goddamn!* He must have thought.
That's me!

Imagining The Worst

Heat-wave psychologists are advising us
That in this week of hundred-plus degrees
We should remind ourselves of colder spells.
The estuaries from the garden hose
That carve small gullies inbetween the corn,
Clear jewels of sweat that bead the water glass,
Blue dollops on a coat of Turtle Wax,
These all should take the form of winter rain.
But there are things that haunt me worse than heat
Which given half the chance I'd will away.

A girlfriend told this story once: one night,
While dusting off a mantelpiece, she tipped
The silver urn which held her mother's ashes.
She started sweeping up and found burnt chips
Of bone and teeth filtering through the silt.
And now, in nightmares, fires swirl her up;
She screams from her sleep and for days remains
Convinced that we are nothing more than ash.

Somewhere, in this same heat, she's spent the night
With someone else. Though nothing is certain,
They may have drifted from their dreams, made love,
And, giddy from exhaustion, laughed their way
Back into sleep, while I strain hard to hear

The soft cascading of an alpine stream,
As children thrash in shallow pools that form
Along the gutters as a hydrant drains.
As for the shrill screams coming from next door
Or wailing sirens in the streets, I'm not
Exactly certain what to make of them.

Buddy Check

Reflected clouds that skim along the lake
Dissolve in all the pandemonium—
They break down to patchy bits of silver
When campers pierce the water's glassy membrane.
Around the docks these boys don't have much sense;
They punch and shove and force each other under.
The lifeguard calls them out when things have gone
Too far. They swish up from the icy water
And count off heads in pairs of glazed and pebbled
Bodies. He wants the numbers synchronized
And loud, and when they botch it he fills them in
On how long he'll wait for their precision—
Forever, of course, if it takes till then.
Behind mirrored glasses from his perch,
He's obsessed with making them get it right
The way my mother insists that I get right
The names of those she's lost in the past.
Carlota. Dorothy. Jane. Claude. And others.
She recites the names as if they could trigger
An instant sorrow in me, but they don't.
Most I've forgotten. Some I never met.
She wants me to feel her grief and I should,
But she fears that I'll slip from her too,
And won't let me forget that those ghosts
Are her life. It's morbid, and like a child

I refuse to get it right. In all the times
I've listened to her hold those people close
And given only deadly silence back,
I wish I could just once, between us, find
A soul to praise or one to be forgiven.

To Charcot: A Letter Never Posted

Sigmund Freud, October, 1886

Blue has spilled across the sky in Vienna
As autumn nears and thumbs the edges of
The birch trees. This month has caught me idle,
Infatuated with the birth of colors
And the dry, timber scent of fallen leaves.

A painter from the square has made our acquaintance.
He calls late in the afternoons. Inevitably—
You know how they can be—he visits through
The dinner hour. Road lamps spurt
And flicker on and he is still with us,
Soiled boots kicked up on the davenport,
Combing his fingers through a greasy beard.

Well into night, our leaded windows provide,
After our guest has chosen to depart,
A rippled view of streetlight and motion
While upstairs, beneath the canopy,
My wife sleeps, entwined perhaps in dreams
Of that painter's sable brush as it swirls
The dark, amber nipple on her portrait.

She leaves me to myself. Angry and brooding.
Jealous, she says, *simply of an idea.*
But what does she know of ideas? I've seen
Her eyes connect with those of other men.
That artist! I cannot hope to counter him.
He brims with such a mystery,
And I am just a scientist,

Though when the choice is mine there is a brief
And pitiful satisfaction in leaving her
Dangling in the quiet of slumber. Each night
I walk the stairs and invariably touch the spots
That will not let me go unnoticed.
Spiteful wood that will not make a sound
When the cat scurries up the steps!
But when my feet go plodding up the boards
There isn't a single stair which doesn't creak.

And it makes me feel more naked—knowing
That she rarely wakes, regardless of my
Introspective clamor. But this is worthless;
It does not matter if she turns to meet me
Or if she keeps her back to me all night,
Because there is a separate life in sleep,
More beautiful than she. Servile and perfect.

Lear's Shadow

With every swipe the amber chips
Zipped into the air as I heaved,
Hauled back, and swung through the bottles
I jammed between two cinder blocks.
I liked the pop and arcing spray
Of broken glass which seemed to drop
Its shower down into itself,
Into the shadow of the forest edge.
I hammered away until I heard
My father's *Dammit!* and felt his hand
Clap against my backside, and jerk
Me howling through our neighbor's yard.

This morning when my father called
His voice was shrill and warbling, thrilled
With the guiltless thrill of love and time.
All thunder gone from that other man
Who couldn't stop to catch his tongue
When I, tears streaming, began to stuff
The necessary things I'd need—
Some shirts, a pair of underpants—
Into a denim duffel bag.
At eight years old when I yammered out
That I was running away from home,
The man who felt he had to say
He'd gladly help me pack.

Damnation of the Sun

It's easy to condemn him, another boy
Who merely disobeyed, so taken by
The rapture of his flight he couldn't stop,
A cool wind at his temple, his breastbone flecked
With grains of sand. As the great wings began
To drip, the feathers dry and singe, before
The headlong tumble to a tranquil sea,
One hopes, at least, at last he understood.
His father, though, who watched his only son
Become a scratch that marred the water's jade,
Would never comprehend how, all at once,
As Icarus fell by, he could desire
To love *and* thrash his rowdy child to death.

Camp Chase Confederate Cemetery

Columbus, Ohio

Enameled by the late June sun,
The clean white headstones lean and lurch,
And though they've been engraved to last
The names have slowly begun to slur.

In a creeping stain of maple shade
My aunt kneels down, begins to make
A charcoal rubbing of his grave
To prove my great-great grandfather's

Been found. These limestone tablets ride
The tilt and buckle of the earth;
They melt a little more each rain.
There seems so much to talk about.

Tunis Muncie. The family tree.
Two thousand soldiers at our feet.
Lost tongues forget their last remarks
In the rigid aisles of the dead,

And silences repeat themselves
From rock to chiseled rock, while all
These tombs remain unshaken by
What has and has not yet been said.

Part III

Epilogue

Because the guests have all gone home,
And sunlight sculpts its late geometries
Across the littered lawn, because
The time for such simplicities is rare,
I'm sitting in a high-backed wicker chair
As summer ends. The tireless bees
That make the apple branches hum
Have found the garnish tray. They come

In pairs, grow drunk on sprigs of mint
And lemon wedges, then hover off
To work the riches of their sweet tree.
I'm thinking of our neighbor Franklin Sloane,
Who spent this August afternoon
Persuading someone else's wife to walk
The nature trail that skirts the lake,
And of the lovely Mrs. Chase, who sat

In this same high-backed wicker chair,
Braiding and unbraiding her gold hair,
While Sloane persuaded her. Between the pines
A brightly sequined water shines
And they may be there still, reluctantly
Departing from their shore, as small masts,
Like tired arms of metronomes,
Rock mildly in the geriatric wake

Of a pontoon boat that prowls the lake.
And whether they regard their fall
As frill or something more profound,
I cannot say; it is no matter.
The saw-toothed shadows of the ferns distend.
A mound of cocktail ice grows clear
Beneath the boxwoods where it was pitched
Like some dismantled, melting chandelier.

I regret to tell you, Mrs. Chase,
You've left your pocketbook behind;
It darkens by the cord of winter wood.
A folding chair out on the grass,
Where your fine yellow sweater hangs,
Enjoys a soft, cashmere embrace
And evening's cloak-work steals the other half
Of your already half-forgotten face.

The City Park

Advancing with the subtlety of moss,
A plush fringework of green has smudged across
The canopy of interlacing limbs.
Throughout this wilderness of antonyms,
The logs that line the slow bend in the creek,
Still heavy from the rains of late last week,
Conduct a steady forfeiture of souls.
Oak leaves, like old, forgotten parchment scrolls,
Suggest the leathered scent of something brown
And conjure up where they decay and drown,
Though it is undeniably mid-May,
Faint whisperings of last Thanksgiving Day.

Bowed down in solemn prayer to stream and stone,
Each one of us pretends to be alone
Or someplace he is not, and overlooks
Corroded cans, crushed bottle glass, matchbooks,
A treasury of foils, some half-inch nails.
A honeysuckle flies two paper sails
That bear the headlines of a Sunday *Times*,
By now a blurry register of crimes
And abstract politics. We see instead
The gilded blade of sunlight overhead
That slices through the forest roof, or pause

To hear the water's constant, soft applause
And watch the creek unravel as it runs,
Its rapids spangled with a thousand suns.

Last month, the body of a child was found
At this trail's end, under a shallow mound
Of twigs and leaves. For nights his neighbors held
A vigil where, today, two workmen weld
The swingset and a massive Junglegym
A local church will dedicate to him.
The men, amid a blossoming of sparks,
Construct from elbows, straightaways, and arcs
A thing of endless possibilities,
As couples pass, identifying trees,
Flowers, and indeterminate small birds.
And yet there is a poverty of words
As lilac, Bradford pear, and marigold
Erupt their tender blooms and I behold
A world, though not entirely redeemed,
Somewhat less foul, less ruined than it seemed.

Tabula Rasa

An evening long before you lighted here,
We tipped a bottle to the news and thanked
Our separate heavens that you would be delivered
Unto us, who have analyzed ourselves
And know that we can give a better love
Than the love we sometimes think we got.
Who are convinced that we know most about
What not to do when you will make us cross.
Who can explain the mysteries of things
With greater care and patience, so we think,
Than all the previous academies,
Like why the maple hillside blazes red
Or how, in the blinding chaos of a storm,
Each crystal flake is formed in symmetry.
We've hotly talked it out and pretty much
Agree that you will make a better us
Than us.

        Above the cradle where we cast
The shadows of ourselves, we ask that you
Somehow overlook the faults in us
That we could not let pass in other folks,
And if you have a gripe that you be kind—
More so than we could ever hope to be.
And for your own sake keep this day in mind,

Locked in the labyrinth of your memory,
How you have stifled every one of us,
Each a self-proclaimed Prometheus,
Reducing all our polysyllables
To nothing more than soft and burbling coos.

Watching Tennis at the U.S. Open

> Who that shall point as with a wand, and say
> "This portion of the river of my mind
> Came from yon fountain"?
>   —Wordsworth, *The Prelude*

From two rows below two hundred rows above,
Under the silent racks of stadium lights
Thrusting upward and bending into dark,
The tops of heads are mostly what we watch
While down below a Lilliputian battle
Flares between two feverish points of white.

Divorced from storm or calm inside each skull,
Through churning braids and flaxen, clutching strands,
These styled heads become synecdoches—
From perfect ace to the cross-court-cross-face,
To daring high and wicked top-spin lobs,
And men spread thin, driven to ground-stroke games—

As tennis, a sport the fashion-minded love,
Is mirrored well among the many coifs.
What furtive streams meander deep beneath
These highly contemplative plots of hair?
The laundry list. The job. The rising rent.
Inviolate rills of thought that mostly lead

To sex, and vexing pangs of shame about
The thoughts of sex. What pools collect wherein
We compose, destroy, and recompose ourselves
As if we were before the bathroom mirror?
(In such a pond did sweet Narcissus find
His wriggling image ungraspably unkind!)

Though we may never know the bubbling source
Or trace the river to its upland spring,
It makes a person want to stop and think.
But in that moment when he's nailed it down,
Before he grips the meaning in his hands,
His consciousness goes rippling down the stream.

Invective

to a football coach

This pillar of our great society
Who sees not sunlight on the autumn grass
Nor marvels at the fires in the trees
When mid-October comes, knows what he knows.
He has a way with motivating boys,
Believes that war brings out the best in man,
And ranks his plays among the likes
Of Shakespeare, Wilde, Brecht, and Sophocles.

May he be tongue-tied grappling for clichés,
Continue packing on ten pounds a year,
Find groundhogs digging up his summer squash,
And strain to scratch his hinder part without
His play book, eight assistants, and a rake.

A Game of Chess

Bobby Fischer not only plans to defy
a U.S. Government warning against
playing a $5 million chess match
in Yugoslavia, yesterday he spat on it.
       —Associated Press

On blonde and walnut varnished squares,
A parlor game of metaphor
That shrinks to scale our politics,
Social orders, and thirst for war,

The master holds the reins on logic.
He views the world in monochrome,
A dioramic match of chess,
And makes of thought a fancy home.

While ordinary days transpire
Inside his cunning head of state
He rules a mute constituency
Which passively concedes he's great.

He rubs his bearded chin and squints
To scan his kingdom as it sprawls
Across the checkered land. The play
Of light upon those marble skulls

Could hardly heat the cockles of
A colder dignitary's heart.
But even he must shed his robes
To face the life outside his art

And demonstrate without a sweat
The sad duplicity of man,
How he can blindly be at once
Both Prospero and Caliban.

Trading Miseries

Beneath the nimbus clouds of barroom smoke
They rode the gentle swell of happy hour
And conjured up with every whiskey sour
A sadder tale than what the others spoke.

Through wretched health, divorce, and calumny,
Each warbled out his own pathetic song,
Assuring his partners, as the bar was long,
No man could be more miserable than he.

To punctuate his life among the dregs
And post as lowest scoundrel in the joint,
One jabbed his hairy index out to point
At a corner dog that licked between its legs.

He claimed it'd been so long since he made love
He often wished that he could do the same;
It was a want he would not try to name,
A plight he could not hope to rise above.

And he with bleak and drunken tale of woe
Sent each one peering deep into his glass
To find an ache in there that could surpass
The pang of this man's harsh and luckless blow.

As streetlight spears began to softly pierce
The foggy, darkling tavern windowpane
One slobbered out, in loserly disdain,
I think that dog would bite you something fierce!

A Lesson Lost

Dazzled, when time had siphoned from the clock,
They wept as they had seen it done before,
As if it were the universe's edge
On which they played and lost that final game.
The fights. The faint blue smell of hockey ice.
It got me going too, apocalypse
And all, until a nearby, prescient fan,
Who didn't say the things I might have thought—
How winning's never taught us very much,
Or the universe has many edges still—
Scratched his cheek and said, *Once in a while,*
It does the little bastards good to lose.

Accidental Walks

On winter nights the deer sneak from the woods
To chew the fringes of the younger pines.
Hoofprints etch across the glistening yard

A travelogue of where they've come and gone.
Brushing up against our world of sleep—
The black and silent house—they leave behind

Only the ideas of where they've roamed
Crushed into the thick and silver field.
The mystery of all the tracks they cast

Is in the gift of knowing where they've been
While we were rapt in business not unlike
Their own, traveling through the dark of dreams

And separately convinced that where we stray
Will never be retraced to where we start.
Side by side, we leave each other there

Perhaps for better things, or fantasies
That love and kindness will not let us speak
Out loud. And through the mist we make our way,

Always, always returning to this home
To the usual us with sour breath
And the warm hands that ache to touch in sleep

The body that the other leaves behind.
The deer are careless with the clues they leave;
Across the snowy night they tramp their paths

While we go undetected on our jaunts
Of shameful lust and cold uncertainty.
It's good to know that we will never have

To answer for the sins we perpetrate
On unsuspecting others when we ourselves
Are also unsuspecting. But more than that,

We'll never have to justify to Jack,
The insomniac who lives three doors away,
Just why he caught a glimpse of us in line

Beneath the all-night supermarket glare
With a pack of Camels and a quart of beer,
Stripped down to nothing but our underwear.

Blue Pool

The fence, shrubs, and pump house floated cleanly,
Reflecting where the wind had cast their shapes
In chipped and rippled likenesses before.
Two lovers sat along the tiled ledge,
Beguiled by their azure counterparts.
Somewhere a thrush had dropped its watery call
When suddenly a diving board's report
Shivered the air and sunlit afternoon.
A diver darting through the blue dispersed
The pump house, shrubs, and fence, the lovers too,
In undulating, dark transparency,
Replacing what at once had been so true
With one great mass of prismed helices,
Drowning deeper than mirrors ever go.

Part IV

Still Life in Pencil

We render into different shades of smoke
This tabletop in lonely disarray,
Its honey-colored, artificial oak,
Assorted fruits, and silver serving tray.

The scavenger who's played this random hand
Now walks the room; from time to time he shows
He's done a sketch, so we might understand
The rumpled apron's flows and counterflows,

Or that each object is a source of light,
Both wrought-iron urn and the fluted champagne glass;
The eggplant should presume to glow despite
Its closeness to the bowl of dimpled brass.

So we must learn to squint, to scrutinize,
To choose what falls within our timid scope,
And if we plan to chart the rose's rise,
It is likely we will forego the hope

Of also capturing the burnished pear
That leans beside the silver serving tray
And mocks a thoroughly indifferent stare.
The woman sitting half the room away

Does not suspect a thing, but I've given up
On wrestling with the lines, the urn's eclipse
And how it clouds the cracked, blue coffee cup.
These tedious and sad relationships

Are not enough to keep me from the thought
Of how her frenzied mane of hair might look
If it were shaken from its ribbon's knot.
It would, I think, run like a sunlit brook

Across her shoulder, collarbone, and breast,
Accentuating her athletic form....
But I should leave this daydream unconfessed.
There lurks in all this gray a brewing storm.

My figures lurch. The apron overflows.
All things proportionately disagree,
And from its cockeyed, unrepentant pose,
That pear has turned its blasted stare on me.

Aquarium

Tucked neatly in the shattered hull,
Each relic of the clipper's wreck
Has settled in its resting place
Below the fissured quarterdeck:
The treasure chest, the smiling skull,
      A sextant in its case.

A diver, tethered by a hose,
And brandishing his fishing spear,
Is arrested in an armored stride.
He's come for coins, a souvenir,
Perhaps a book of captain's prose.
      Along the starboard side

An anchor curls its iron arms;
Fingers of seaweed duck and twist
Where a bearded goldfish ambles through,
A solemn existentialist,
Inspects the mast, the ripped yardarms,
      Then wriggles out of view,

His tailfin rippling like a flame.
He threads a fluid course between
The ship's bare rib cage and the rocks.

He's lost inside a scripted scene
Where suffering forgets its shame.
     The very sea it mocks

Flexes, slides, and rolls back on itself
Two rain-glazed miles away from here.
Queer, scattered shadows haunt this house
As whitecaps whittle at the pier
And carve a deeper coastal shelf.
     Her half-unbuttoned blouse.

The silver necklace on her throat.
Who would not choose to drown in this?
The diver breathes an endless strand
Of pearls and prowls a bright abyss,
Forsakes the solace of his boat
     For sunken contraband.

He learns an old curriculum;
We watch the toy-store ebbs and flows,
Entranced as if by greater waves,
And marvel how this ocean shows
That some grave waters can become
     Not kind, but gentler graves.

The Nightly News

Today, in the war-torn state, the nightly news
Reports the dead have numbered only one,
Which isn't bad, one has to think, for the land
Ravaged in shards and dust and overrun

By love of country. The television glows
With puddled streets, abandoned garden carts,
And the bullet-stippled window of a shop—
The landscape of a million hollow hearts.

The young married couple squander the night
Bickering over their standard of living
And how even making love has turned out sour.
Between the pair they've given up on giving.

They go bitterly through their dinner time,
Riddled by silence and the anchor's voice
Which tells them in a stark non sequitur
How they bear all their grievances by choice.

But all of this is nature's sleight:
While through this scene an abstract ache goes throbbing,
In the unremitting fever of some dark
The mother of that casualty lies sobbing.

The First Returning Trees

He pondered often how the oaks returned
Mossy-topped at April's end, even though
They'd only see their leaves in autumn burned

On a single, cold October afternoon
As if their yearly solitary fate
Were to have their papery mischief strewn

And scattered on the vast, indifferent earth.
How positively sad it seemed to him,
While cogitating on this springtime birth,

That lives of leaves so closely mirror ours,
From emerald bud to dull and withered frond,
In passing through their turns on oak tree towers,

To find so near the end that all they've made
As each by each they plunge from jutting limb,
Is nothing more than ever-shrinking shade.

The Last Day of School

Behind the picture windows of the school
Where chalky afternoons are often spent
Solving for x, or hovering above
The gurgling chemistry experiment,

The students pace the labyrinth of the halls,
Trampling the fretwork of the granite floors
And file into their curricular vaults
To learn the ancient origins of wars

Or trace the constellations of the skies
On a blackened map of sparks where they must sift
Great mythic silhouettes from lesser stars
In practicing the awesome human gift

Of seeing likenesses in unlike things.
And in the separate chambers where they're taught
The countless threads of fact, their task becomes
To weave a solitary rope of thought

And grasp the common rhythms of the world;
To see in Hamlet's ceaseless, wrenching grief
About the universal laws of change
A nexus to the stoical belief

Which Heraclitus long ago proposed
When he, two thousand years before, defined
An earth that's ever forging on its way,
And said, *We're always leaving here behind.*

Outside, the dogwood sentries hold their posts
As on this afternoon the pupils pass
A final time beneath those knotted boughs
And exit tentatively free of class.

The principal will see the stragglers run
To board the last, departing yellow bus,
And ponder outwardly on how the x
We spend our whole lives solving for is us.

Behold, the Storm Departs

The water globes collect and roll
From fingertips of sagging leaves
And asphalt pavements sweat their mist
As overhead the sky receives
Return of its recycled rain.
Between two listing clothesline posts
Three habits hang and snap their sleeves
In the remnant winds of an August storm
Like shoulder-shrugging holy ghosts.

Slate blue thunderheads sail eastward
And I, a little sad with scotch,
On a path of dim, corroded stones,
Crouch by the churchyard gates to watch
The pageantry of summer's dusk.
A mower works the fading light
To shave the still-remaining swatch
Of uncut grass, and dragonflies
Slice zigzags in their spastic flight.

The double-jointed clergymen
Suspended on their laundry wire
Break at the elbows, snake their spines,
And simultaneously conspire
To rip themselves from their dangling lot.

As now a million days conclude,
The cock which tops the chapel spire
Rocks tightly on his axis and jabs
His beak in copper certitude.

Yet even he will change his mind.
Faroff, thunder growls; cold bells chime.
Sparrows over the puddled land
Ride gusts in dogfight pantomime.
To make this mean is not the point,
Or render from the blue landscape
A gilded code or paradigm
As stillness grows and the darkening world
Is blanketed in shades of grape.

At night, in awe of summer's rage,
When heat gathers in folds and pleats,
I churn and thrash the bed to find
Cool pockets in the cotton sheets,
Thumb sweat from my temple and think,
For once, *Thank God I am alone.*
But even as each fan blade beats
The hot, black air across the room
I hear in that propeller's groan

The racket of bedsprings, sighs, and sobs,
And it's the thought of love that haunts
Me from my sleep until I've forged
A stockpile of unanswered wants
For women, power, wealth, and time.
Each lust begets another lust.
Heat lightning, nightly, flares and taunts
Dry grass that bristles underfoot
And a garden plot of scab and dust.

Ripples of jasper light the clouds.
Stray lozenges of water pop
Against the sill to punctuate
A thirst with every errant drop.
But that is all the sky will give.
No tantrum, prayer, or harsh complaint
Can drive desire to its stop,
Erase insomnia, or cleanse
An air that hangs as thick as paint.

Both form and light depart this day;
An earth scrubbed clean of August grit
Remains where once the hammering rains
And thunderbolts admonished it.

And I am murmured home toward sleep
Past churchyard, stones, and wind-whipped frocks.
As though they will not ever quit,
Clear rivulets beside the walk
Rattle and click like tireless clocks.

Cinema Americain

The outcast in the end had gained,
From those who had excluded him,
A sudden gush of love and thanks.
And the girl for whom he had longed two hours
Stretched across the hood of the beat-up coupe
That won the race and chased the villain's
Lackeys out to the town's dusty edge.
She, in sure repose, beneath
A beech tree's shade and checkered by
The sunlight cutting through the leaves,
In body language said to him,
We're sorry to have made you feel
So helplessly inadequate
In your up-to-now feeble life.
And he accepted the remorse,
Although unspoken, and the two
Pitched themselves into the car
And drove somewhere to carry on
Our dark imaginings. Smiling,
The last we saw, they left us there
To contemplate their lives and ours.

Through tangled crowd and lobby-light,
We left that perfect place behind,
Agreeing, every one of us,

That had we been those characters
Things would not have ended such.
The engine would have sputtered out;
The villains would have done us in.
And though we're far too smart to buy
Into all that drippy schmaltz,
We keep on paying for the stuff,
Privately aching for the day
This inadvertent world returns our love.

Dontophobic

He rocks the pointer back and forth,
Plucking upon the ivory stones
And periodically gets stuck
Where two bicuspids clash or in
The soft patch of some cavity.
My right eye clenched and left eye
Screaming wide, I answer this with gasps,
Dollops of breath in unformed words,
Cursing the pain and cursing him.
And as he digs along
The borderlines of gum and tooth
He sees in there a simple mouth.
But this is where the troubles start,
When words burst out and make us fierce
With hate or joy. Fear or lust.

Sometimes, alone and softly drunk,
I've called friends to say how much
I love them. *Yes*, they know, and love
Me too. After hanging up,
That phrase wisps into silence
And I want it back because
It seems as if I've burdened them,
Not with something false or common,
But prompted them to offer up

A piece of themselves. Anger's not
Much different. Once or twice a week
The next-door neighbor staggers home
Stiff with rage to yell at his wife.
Through windows and trellis vines
Their fights divide the summer air.

She talks of hate as if she needs
To hear it back. Perhaps she does.
All night long they take nothing back
And the muscles down my spine go rigid,
Wrenching when I hear his ghostly sobs.

The dentist sees a mouth—the X-ray's
Milky outline of my jaw—
Snaps a rubber glove from his hand,
Offers me a new toothbrush,
And says it all looks fine in there.
While scuffing down his silent hall
I search for comfort in his words.

The Dog Laments His Day

The house gives way to dimmer shades of dim
As tree limbs quiver and a passing storm
Unloads its tantrum as I wait for him.
Although I've often promised my reform,
I've rifled through his freshly laundered socks,
Played *sliders* on the Oriental rug,
Shredded tissues, and tipped the litter box.
The cat, my Super Ego, waxes smug
At all the mischief I cannot repair
And snakes her tail high on the mantelpiece.
As always, after rage there comes despair.
Outside, dark starlings ride the wind's increase;
The cold rain water trickles from the eaves
And I sink low to watch the trembling leaves.

Biographical Information

Daniel Anderson's poems have appeared in *Poetry, The New Republic, Raritan, The Southern Review,* and *Southwest Review* among other places. He holds an M.A. from Johns Hopkins University and a B.A. from the University of Cincinnati. He was a recipient of a 1995 fellowship from the New Jersey State Council on the Arts. He currently lives in Morristown, New Jersey where he teaches English and creative writing at Delbarton School.